The New Homemade Dog Treat Cookbook

Simple and Delicious Recipes That Your Dog Will Love

Nora Turner

Disclaimer 2021 – Nora Turner

The following Book is reproduced below with the goal of providing information that is as accurate and reliable as possible. Regardless, purchasing this Book can be seen as consent to the fact that both the publisher and the author of this book are in no way experts on topics discussed within and that any recommendations or suggestions that are made herein are for entertainment purposes only. Information in the following pages is broadly considered a truthful and accurate account of facts, as such, any inattention, use, or misuse of information in question by the reader will render any resulting actions solely under their purview.

There are no scenarios in which the publisher or the original author of this work can be in any fashion deemed liable for any hardship or damages that may befall them after undertaking information described herein. Additionally, the information in the following pages is intended only for informational purposes and should thus be thought of as universal. As befitting its nature, it is presented without assurance regarding its prolonged validity or interim quality. Trademarks that are mentioned are done without written consent and can in no way be considered an endorsement from trademark holder.

All information is available for educational and informational purposes only. Food sensitivity is a reaction to one or more ingredients, contained in food, that the dog's body does not tolerate well. It is also referred to as an "adverse reaction to food." The problem is quite common and may depend on an immune or non-immune based reaction. Food sensitivity is a problem that varies from individual to individual, but although each dog is a case in point, intolerances generally involve commonly used ingredients to which the animal has already been exposed, such as beef, chicken, dairy products or wheat. Frequent diarrhea, vomiting, especially just after eating, could be symptoms of food sensitivities. Therefore, it is recommended to test any recipe contained in this manual, only under the advice and suggestion of your trusted veterinarian.

Table of Contents

INTRODUCTION 11
    WHY CARBOHYDRATES ARE BAD FOR DOGS 19

ACE'S FAVORITE CHEESY DOG BISCUITS 23

ALFALFA HEARTS 25

ALFIE AND ARCHIE'S DOG BISCUITS 26

AN APPLE A DAY DOG TREAT 28

APPLE CINNAMON DOGGIE BISCUITS 29

APPLE CRUNCH PUPCAKES 31

AUNT BIANCA'S DOG BISCUITS 32

BABY FOOD DOGGIE COOKIES 34

BACON BITES 35

BACON BITS FOR DOGS 37

BAKER'S BAGELS 38

BARF BREAKFAST (MED SIZE DOG) 39

BARF DINNER (MED SIZE DOG) 41

BARKING BARLEY BROWNIES 42

BASENJI STEW 43

BEEF AND RICE MOOCHIES 45

BEEF TWISTS 46

BIRTHDAY CAKE FOR PUPS 47

BISCUITS FOR DOGS	49
BJ'S PEANUTTY PUPCICLES	50
BONE A FIDOS	51
BONE BONANZA	55
BOO'S BISCUITS	56
BOW WOW BISCUITS	57
BOW WOW BURRITOS	59
BREAD MACHINE DOG BISCUITS	61
BREATH BUSTERS BISCUITS	64
BUDDY BOYS DOG BISCUITS	65
BULLDOG BANANA BITES	66
BULLDOG BROWNIES	67
CANINE CARROT COOKIES	69
CANINE COOKIES #1	70
CANINE COOKIES #2	71
CANINE COOKIES #3	73
CANINE MEAT AND GRAIN MENU	74
CAROB CORNERED CRUNCHIES	75
CHAMPION CHEESE & VEGGIES CHEWS	77
CHEESE AND BACON DOG BISCUITS	78
CHEESE AND GARLIC DOG COOKIES	79
CHEESE N GARLIC BITES	81

CHEESEY DOG COOKIES	82
CHEESY CARROT MUFFINS	83
CHEWY CHEESY CHIHUAHUA PIZZA	85
CHICKEN FLAVORED DOG BISCUITS	87
CHICKEN GARLIC BIRTHDAY CAKE	90
CHOW CHOW CHICKEN	91
CHOW CHOW STEW	93
CLASSIC CANINE COOKIES	95
CORGI CRUMPETS	98
DARLENE'S FAVORITE DOG COOKIE	99
NOTE	102

Introduction

Preparing homemade dog food is the best way to save money and to ensure your four-legged friend a wholesome and healthy diet. After learning commercial dog foods are rich in harmful additives, many owners have started preparing meals at home. Other owners, on the other hand, cook food for their dogs for health reasons. In short, whatever the reason, it is very easy to prepare a delicious meal for your dog.

Canine nutrition

Many people think that dogs should only eat protein. False. Dogs, just like us humans, need a variety of meats, starches and vegetables to meet their nutritional needs. If dogs ate only protein, they would not be able to enjoy the benefits of vitamins, thus causing thyroid problems. If they do not get enough protein, they could suffer from poor immune function, muscle breakdown, and blood disorders. Hence, it is vital that the diet is balanced. Veterinarians recommend following percentages: 40% protein, 50% vegetables and 10% starch.

Ingredients to use

Each food category has a wide range of ingredients to choose from. The important thing is that the ingredient is fresh and does not contain additives.

Protein

People usually think that dogs only eat beef, but there are many other sources of protein. Muscle or organ meat is perfect. Use liver in moderation as animal liver may contain impurities. You can use these protein sources depending on availability, cost:

- Beef - ground or shredded
- Turkey - easy to find and digest, as well as being cheap
- Chicken - like turkey, cheap and easy to find
- Lamb
- Fish - mackerel or herring, but not more than once or twice a week
- Beans - pinto beans or red kidney beans, but they must not replace meat proteins
- Eggs - in moderation

Food Vegetables

Dogs can eat a lot of vegetables. However, some are to be avoided. Here are the ones they can eat:

- Carrots
- Green beans
- Broccoli - they cause gas
- Cauliflower - they cause gas
- Spinach
- Peas
- Celery
- Cucumbers
- Pumpkin

Carbohydrates

Carbohydrates contain vitamins that are very important for dogs. They also provide the right amount of fiber which aids digestion. Here is what they are:

- Brown rice
- Potatoes - must be cooked

- Pasta - without salt or oil
- Oats
- Sweet potatoes

<u>Ingredients to avoid</u>

People mistakenly think that dogs can eat anything. In fact, some foods that are normal for us could be lethal to dogs. Do not include these foods in your dog's food preparation:

- Chocolate
- Onions
- Raisins
- Avocado
- Grapes
- Hazelnuts and macadamia nuts
- Coffee
- Spices like curry or paprika
- Raw yeast dough

Of course, you should not use any ingredients that have gone bad or contain mold. The golden rule is that you should never give your dog what you would never eat.

Garlic is a controversial ingredient, especially when raw. Despite this, many dog food houses include a pinch or two of cooked garlic in their preparations. Check with your vet to clear up any concerns.

<u>Ingredients to limit</u>

Some ingredients can be taken by dogs, but only in limited quantities:

- Butter
- Salt
- Dairy product
- Cooking oils
- Corn

While wild wolves eat raw food, the same is not true for your dog. To be safe, food must be cooked properly to eliminate the risk of diseases such as salmonella, present in raw chicken. It is eliminated only by cooking food until it reaches a temperature of about 176° F.

Here is an easy and simple recipe. When preparing your meal, remember the percentages we talked about earlier: 40% protein, 50% vegetables and 10% starch.

- ✓ Fill a large saucepan with water and turn on the stove over low heat.

- ✓ Wash and cut the potatoes in their skins. Put them in the water and cook for ten minutes.

- ✓ Add ground turkey, veal, or chicken (boneless) to the pot.

- ✓ Add fresh or frozen vegetables. Try to vary, for example you can put carrots, peas and spinach.

- ✓ Add some pasta or oats and let it boil for 10-15 minutes.

- ✓ Remove the pot from the heat and let it cool. Divide the food into portions and freeze it in special containers so that you always have a ready meal.

Fresh vegetables usually cost less than canned or frozen vegetables and contain more vitamins when harvested at the right time (from your garden or bought from a trusted farmer). If you need to buy canned vegetables, be sure to choose those with less salt.

<u>Tips for preparing your dog's meal</u>

- ✓ Prepare food in large enough quantities that you can only do it once a week.

- ✓ Beware of using your leftovers. Do they contain butter, seasonings or other ingredients that are bad for the dog? If the answer is yes, do not use them.

- ✓ Always ask your veterinarian for advice before making any changes to your dog's diet. Also ask if the dog should take supplements.

Even if you do not always can prepare food for your dog, you can do it occasionally to ensure a genuine, healthy alternative to his usual meal.

Why carbohydrates are bad for dogs

Certain types of carbohydrates are good for your dog's health. However, not all carbohydrates are created equal and there are many that are generally unhealthy for your dog's body. These carbohydrates are often included in many commercial dog food recipes and should be avoided. It is always recommended to choose the best kibble or a grain-free dog food.

<u>Carbohydrates to Avoid in a Canine Diet</u>

There are two general types of carbohydrate categories that should not be given to dogs: high glycemic index carbohydrates and highly processed carbohydrates.

High-glycemic carbohydrates are foods that can cause your blood sugar to rise immediately after eating them. The glycemic index (GI) classifies the increase in blood sugar level.

The GI ranges for food are:

- ✓ Low: 55 or less
- ✓ Moderate: 56-69
- ✓ High: 70 or more

The foods with higher GI values cause higher and larger blood sugar spikes. The foods with lower GI values cause slower and more moderate increases in blood sugar. In general, foods that are high in blood sugar are not healthy (although there are exceptions).

Why are high GI carbohydrates bad for dogs?

High GI foods are potentially harmful to the body because spikes in blood sugar levels can trigger a chronic (long-term) internal inflammatory response. This chronic inflammation can facilitate a variety of different diseases including diabetes, heart problems, arthritis, cancer and obesity.

High GI foods are commonly found in commercial dog foods, and those to avoid include:

- ✓ Corn, including corn meal and corn derivatives
- ✓ White rice
- ✓ Wheat
- ✓ Sugar in any form (e.g. sugar or sucrose)
- ✓ White potatoes (although potatoes may provide some health benefits, especially for dogs with gastrointestinal or liver problems).

Instead of the above ingredients, look for dog foods that contain healthier and usually low GI foods like cruciferous vegetables, berries, and many other fruits and legumes. When it comes to grains, low GI ones are preferred. Try to purchase sorghum, quinoa, and oats as healthful grain choices.

Highly Processed Carbohydrates

As with humans, highly processed foods will lose their nutritional potency and offer little health benefits to a dog. For example, consider plain white rice, which lacks the nutritional point versus brown rice, which can be a healthy ingredient. In dog foods it is wise to look for foods that are in or near their integral state. As if a high GI food was not enough, the further processing makes many of the ingredients cheaper, the filler ingredients even less appropriate for a dog.

Examples include wheat gluten and corn gluten and corn meal. Avoid these ingredients as they are a sign of an inferior food recipe.

Ace's Favorite Cheesy Dog Biscuits

- 1 1/2 cups whole wheat flour
- 1 1/4 cups grated cheddar cheese
- 1/4 pound margarine -- corn oil
- 1 clove garlic -- crushed
- 1 pinch salt
- 1/4 cup Milk -- or as needed

Grate the cheese into a bowl and let stand until it reaches room temperature. Cream cheese with soft margarine, garlic, salt and flour. Add enough milk to form a ball.

Cool for 1/2 hour. Roll into the flourboard. Cut into a shape and bake at 375 degrees for 15 minutes or until a little chocolate, and firmly. Make 2 to 3 dozen, depending on the size.

Yield: "24 biscuits"

Alfalfa Hearts

- 2 cups whole wheat flour
- 1/2 cup soy flour
- 1 teaspoon bone meal -- optional
- 2 tablespoons nutritional yeast
- 1 tablespoon lecithin -- optional
- 1/2 teaspoon salt
- 1/4 teaspoon garlic powder
- 3 tablespoons alfalfa sprouts -- chopped
- 1 cup brown rice -- cooked
- 3 tablespoons canola oil
- 1/2 cup water

Combine the flour, bone flour, yeast, lecithin, salt, garlic powder and alfalfa leaves. Add the rice and oil. Join well. Add 1/4 cup of water and mix well. Dough must be very easy to handle, not destroyed.

Add more water if necessary, to achieve the right consistency. Light flour, boards or counters and roll out mixture up to 1/4-inch thickness. Cut with cutters 2 and 1/2 inches. Bake at 350-degree for 25 minutes. Make 3 dozen.

Alfie And Archie's Dog Biscuits

- ❖ 2 1/2 cups whole wheat flour
- ❖ 1/2 cup dry milk -- powder
- ❖ 1/2 teaspoon salt
- ❖ 1/2 teaspoon garlic powder
- ❖ 1 teaspoon brown sugar
- ❖ 6 tablespoons beef fat
- ❖ 1 egg -- beaten
- ❖ 1/2 cup ice water

Preheat the oven to 350. Light oil Cake sheet. Combine flour, dry milk, salt, garlic and sugar powder. Cut drippings meat until the mixture resembles corn flour. Mix in egg. Add enough water so the mixture forms a ball.

Use your fingers, apply the mixture to the cake sheet to half an inch. Cut with Cookie Cutter or knife and delete memo. Memo can be formed again and baked.

Bake 25-30 minutes. Remove from the tray and cool on shelf.

An Apple a Day Dog Treat

- ❖ 2 cups whole wheat flour
- ❖ 1/2 cup unbleached flour
- ❖ 1/2 cup cornmeal
- ❖ 1 apple -- chopped or grated
- ❖ 1 egg -- beaten
- ❖ 1/3 cup vegetable oil
- ❖ 1 tablespoon brown sugar, packed
- ❖ 3/8 cup water

Preheat the oven to 350 degrees. Spray Cookie Sheet with the vegetable oil spray. Working surface of light dust with flour. Mix flour and corn mixed bowls. Add apples, eggs, oil, brown sugar and water, mix until mixed well. On the surface of flour, roll the mixture into a 7/8-inch thickness.

Cut with a cake cutter shape and the desired size. Place a snack on the prepared sheet. Bake the oven which is heated 35 to 40 minutes. Turn off the oven. Leave the door closed one hour to treat Crisp. Remove treats from the oven. Save baked food in an airtight container or plastic bag and place it in the refrigerator or freezer. Make 2 to 2 1/2 dozen.

Apple Cinnamon Doggie Biscuits

- ❖ 1 package apple, dried
- ❖ 1 teaspoon Cinnamon -- (I usually just shake some in)
- ❖ 1 Tablespoon parsley, freeze-dried
- ❖ 1 Tablespoon Garlic Powder
- ❖ 1 cup ice water
- ❖ 1/2 cup Corn Oil
- ❖ 5 cups flour
- ❖ 1/2 cup powdered milk
- ❖ 2 large eggs
- ❖ 1 tablespoon corn oil

Place the apple in the food processor so that the pieces are small. Combine in a bowl of all ingredients - can add oil or water if the mixture is too dry. Using rolling pin rolls of dough around 3/16 "thick (can make thinner or thicker).

Using Cookie Cutter - cut into shapes - Place it on cake sheet. Bake at 350 degrees around 20 -25 minutes (to golden).

Note: If you replace eating corn, reduce around 3/4 cups from flour and add corn flour.

Apple Crunch Pupcakes

- 2 3/4 cups water
- 1/4 cup unsweetened applesauce
- 2 tablespoons honey
- 1 medium egg
- 1/8 teaspoon vanilla extract
- 4 cups whole wheat flour
- 1 cup apple, dried
- 1 tablespoon baking powder

Preheat oven to 350 degrees. In a small bowl, mix water, apples, honey, eggs, and vanilla. In large bowl, combine the flour, apple chip, and powder cake. Add melting to dry and mix up until is very mixed well. Pour into an oily muffin pan, bake 1 and 1/4 hour, or until the toothpick is inserted in the middle of coming dry. Store in a closed container.

Make 12 to 14 pupcakes.

Aunt Bianca's Dog Biscuits

- 2 1/2 cups whole wheat flour
- 1/2 cup nonfat dry milk powder
- 1 teaspoon garlic powder
- 1 egg -- beaten

Seasoning: Drippings of meat, broth or water from canned tuna (enough to make a rigid dough). Combine flour, milk powder and garlic powder in a medium-sized bowl. Add the offspring of eggs, spices, and mix by hand. The mixture must be very stiff. If you need to add more flavor.

On the surface of the flour well, scroll the mixture up to 1/4-inch thickness. Cut with your preferred cake cutter.

Place the biscuits on the cake sheet and cake at 350 degrees for 30 minutes.

Baby Food Doggie Cookies

- 3 jars baby food, meat, beef, strained -- *see Note
- 1/4 cup cream of wheat -- *see Note
- 1/4 cup dry milk

Combine ingredients in a bowl and mix well. Roll to the small ball and place it on an oiled cake sheet. Finally, with a fork. Bake Oven 350 degrees which is heated for 15 minutes. Until brown.

Cool on wire shelf and store it in the fridge. Also freezes well.

Note: Carrot food, chicken or beef cow. Replacing wheat germs for wheat cream.

Bacon Bites

- 3 cups whole wheat flour
- 1/2 cup milk
- 1 egg
- 1/4 cup bacon grease -- or vegetable oil
- 1 teaspoon garlic powder
- 4 slices bacon -- crumbled
- 1/2 cup cold water

Mix ingredients together thoroughly. Roll out on a floured surface to 1/2 - 1/4" thickness. Bake for 35-40 minutes in a 325-degree oven.

Bacon Bits for Dogs

- ❖ 6 slices cooked bacon -- crumbled
- ❖ 4 eggs -- well beaten
- ❖ 1/8 cup bacon grease
- ❖ 1 cup water
- ❖ 1/2 cup powdered milk -- non-fat
- ❖ 2 cup graham flour
- ❖ 2 cup wheat germ
- ❖ 1/2 cup cornmeal

Mix ingredients with a strong spoon.

Drop heaping tablespoonfuls onto a greased baking sheet. Bake in a 350 oven for 15 minutes. Turn off oven and leave cookies on baking sheet in the oven overnight to dry out.

Baker's Bagels

- ❖ 1 cup whole wheat flour
- ❖ 1 cup unbleached flour
- ❖ 1 package yeast -- 1/4 ounce
- ❖ 1 cup chicken broth -- warmed
- ❖ 1 tablespoon honey

Heat the oven to 375° F. In a large bowl combine wheat flour with yeast. Add 2/3 cups of chicken and honey broth and beats for about 3 minutes. Gradually add the remaining flour.

Knead dough for a few minutes until smooth and humid, but not wet (use the backup broth as needed).

Cover the mixture and let the break for about 5 minutes. Divide the mixture to around 15-20 pieces, roll over each part into a smooth ball. Punch a hole into each ball with your finger or end of spoon and gently pull the dough so the hole is about an 1/2" wide. Do not be too fussy here, small bagel rises into its shape. Place all the bagels on the cake sheet that is oiled and allowing to rise 5 Minute. Bake for 25 minutes.

Turn off the heat and let the bagel cool in the oven.

BARF Breakfast (med size dog)

- 1/4 cup rolled oats
- 1/2 cup yogurt
- 1/4 cup vegetables -- *see Note
- 250 mgs vitamin C -- for dogs. Crushed
- 1 teaspoon honey
- 1 teaspoon apple cider vinegar
- 1 teaspoon kelp seaweed powder -- *see Note
- 1 teaspoon alfalfa powder -- *see Note
- 1 digestive enzyme -- for dogs Optional
- 1 teaspoon flax seed oil -- *see Note
- 1/4 cup kibble -- optional

Soak rolled oats in yogurt overnight. Mix all ingredients and serve. Add kibble if desired.

Note: shredded, lightly steamed, or pureed, Carrots and celery, spinach, yams and/or broccoli, apples etc.

Note: items can be purchased at health food store or pet store.

BARF Dinner (med size dog)

- 3/4-pound Raw Meat -- *see Note
- 1 egg -- raw
- 1/2 clove garlic -- chopped
- 2 tablespoons yogurt
- 1 teaspoon honey
- 1 tablespoon apple cider vinegar
- 1/2 teaspoon flax seed oil -- *see Note
- 1 teaspoon kelp seaweed powder -- *see Note
- 1 teaspoon alfalfa powder -- *see Note
- 250 mgs vitamin C -- for dogs
- 1/4 cup kibble -- optional

Mix together and serve.

*Note: raw beef chunks (not ground), raw chicken, mackerel, or lamb etc. twice a week use liver or kidney.

Note: found in health food store or pet store

Barking Barley Brownies

- ❖ 1 1/4 pounds beef liver -- or chicken liver
- ❖ 2 cups wheat germ
- ❖ 2 tablespoons whole wheat flour
- ❖ 1 cup cooked barley
- ❖ 2 whole eggs
- ❖ 3 tablespoons peanut butter
- ❖ 1 clove garlic
- ❖ 1 tablespoon olive oil
- ❖ 1 teaspoon salt -- optional

Pre Heat Oven to 350. Liquid liver and garlic in a blender when smooth add eggs and peanut butter. Blend until smooth. In the separate mixing bowl combining wheat germs, the whole wheat flour, and cooked wheat. Add a mixture of processed liver, olive oil and salt. Mix well. Spread the mixture on oily 9x9 cake plate. Bake for 20 minutes or until it is finished.

When cool is cut into pieces that accommodate your doggie size. Store in the fridge or freezer.

Start to complete the time: "0:45"

Basenji Stew

- 4 small parsnip -- **see Note
- 2 whole yellow squash -- cubed
- 2 whole Sweet potatoes -- peeled and cubed
- 2 whole Zucchini -- cubed
- 5 whole tomatoes -- canned
- 1 can garbanzo beans, canned -- *see Note 15 oz
- 1/2 cup Couscous
- 1/4 cup Raisins
- 1 teaspoon Ground coriander
- 1/2 teaspoon Ground turmeric
- 1/2 teaspoon Ground cinnamon
- 1/2 teaspoon Ground ginger
- 1/4 teaspoon Ground cumin
- 3 cups Water -- *see Note

** kohlrabi may be substituted for the parsnips. *Chick-peas *or 3 cups chicken stock

Combine all the ingredients in a large saucepan. Bring to a boil, lower heat, simmer until vegetables are tender, about 30 mins. Place over cook brown rice or barley.

Beef and Rice Moochies

- 1 jar babyfood, dinner, vegetables and beef, strained
- 2 1/2 cups flour, all-purpose
- 1 cup whole wheat flour
- 1 cup rice
- 1 package unflavored gelatin
- 1 whole egg
- 2 tablespoons vegetable oil
- 1 cup powdered milk
- 1 package yeast
- 1/4 cup warm water
- 1 beef bouillon cube

Dissolve yeast in warm water. Mix dry ingredients in a large bowl. Add yeast, eggs, oil, baby food, and bouillon of dissolved beef. Mix well. The mixture will be very dry, knead with hands to form a ball. Roll out on the surface of flour until the thickness of 1/4 inches, cut in a circle of 1 or 2 inches.

Bake on cake sheet that is not oiled 30 minutes at 300 degrees. Store in refrigerator.

Beef Twists

- 3 1/2 cups flour, all-purpose
- 1 cup cornmeal
- 1 package unflavored gelatin
- 1/4 cup milk
- 1 egg
- 1/4 cup corn oil
- 1 jar Baby food, meat, beef, strained
- 1 beef bouillon cube
- 3/4 cup boiling water -- or beef stock

Dissolve Bouillon Cube in water. Filter the dry ingredients in a large bowl. Add milk, eggs, oil, beef and bouillon.

Stir until mixed well. Roll on the flour surface to a thickness of 1/4 inch. Cut in 1/4 inch with a 3-inch strip, rotate each stick 3 changes before placing on the cookie sheet. Bake 35-40 minutes with 400 degrees.

Store in the refrigerator.

Birthday Cake for Pups

- 1 1/2 cups all-purpose flour
- 1 1/2 teaspoons baking powder
- 1/2 cup soft butter
- 1/2 cup corn oil
- 1 jar baby food, meat, beef, strained
- 4 eggs
- 2 strips beef jerky -- (2 to 3)

Heat the oven to 325 degrees. Grease and flour pan bread 8x5x3 inches. Cream butter until smooth. Add corn oil, baby food, and eggs. Mix until smooth.

Mix dry ingredients into a mixture of beef until the mixture is smooth. Crumble beef and folding into a dough. Pour mixture into a loaf pan. Bake 1 hour and 10 minutes. Cool on a 15-minute wire rack. Ice with plain yogurt or cottage cheese.

Save cakes that are not eaten in the fridge.

Biscuits for Dogs

- 1 cup oatmeal -- uncooked
- 1/3 cup margarine
- 1 tablespoon beef bouillon granules
- 5 1/2 cups hot water
- 1 tablespoon garlic powder -- optional
- 3/4 cup powdered milk
- 3/4 cup cornmeal
- 3 cups whole wheat flour
- 1 whole egg -- beaten

Pour hot water on oatmeal, margarine, and bouillon; Let stand for 6 minutes. Stir milk, corn flour, and eggs. Add flour, 1/2 c. at a time; Mix well after each additional.

Royad 3 - 4 minutes., Add more flour needed to make the dough very rigid. Roll or tap the mixture to 1/2 ". Cut into a dog bone shape with Cookie Cutter.

Bake at 325 degrees for 50 minutes. At fast roasting it makes it possible to cool and dry up hard. Store in a container.

BJ'S Peanutty Pupcicles

- 1 ripe banana
- 1/2 cup peanut butter
- 1/4 cup wheat germ
- 1/4 cup chopped peanuts

Mash banana and peanut butter stir in wheat germ.

Chill 1 hour. Place in container, store in refrigerator or freezer.

Bone A Fidos

- 2 1/4 teaspoons Dry yeast
- 1/4 cup warm water -- (liquid measure)
- 1 Pinch sugar
- 3 1/2 cups All-purpose flour
- 2 cups Whole wheat flour
- 2 cups Cracked wheat
- 1 cup Rye flour
- 1/2 cup Nonfat dry milk
- 4 teaspoons Kelp powder
- 4 cups Beef broth -- or chicken

GLAZE:

- 1 large egg
- 2 tablespoons Milk

Equipment:

Cake sheets that are coated with parchment or aluminum foil; dough grinder; 3-3 1/2 "bone cutter or 2 1/2" round the cookie cutter. Place 2 ovens shelves in the top and bottom of the oven. Heat the oven to 300 degrees.

Sprinkle dry yeast or yeast compressed on water (110 degrees if the yeast is dry, 100 degrees if yeast compressed). Add a pinch of sugar and let yeast sit in a draft free place for 10-20 minutes. The mixture must be full of bubbles. If not, the yeast is too old to be useful.

In a large bowl, put all the dry ingredients and stir to blend. Add mixed yeast and 3 cups of broth. Use your hands, in a bowl, mix to form the dough, add more broth if needed to make the mixture smooth and chewy. Half of the batch at one time, knead mixture briefly at a light connection. (Keep second batter batch covered with moist towels while forming and cutting fast.)

Roll out the dough into an 18 x 13 x 1/4" rectangle. Cut it into desired shapes, using a 3 - 3 1/2-inch bone cutter or a 2 1/2-inch round cookie cutter. Re-roll the scraps. Repeat the procedure with the remaining dough.

For attractive luster, shake light eggs and milk. Brush glaze on cookies. Bake for 45 to 60 minutes or until chocolate and firmly.

Even to roast twist cake sheet from top to bottom ¾ of the road through baking period. Use a small metal spatula, tilt or turner pancake to transfer cookies to the wire rack to cool completely.

Store in an airtight container at room temperature. The dough must be used immediately.

Grilled cookies will be saved for months. Let the cake sheet cool completely between batches.

Bone Bonanza

- 1/2-pound ground beef -- uncooked
- 1/4 cup chicken broth
- 1/3 cup black beans, cooked -- mashed
- 1/3 cup cottage cheese
- 1 teaspoon soy sauce

Combine ground meat and chicken broth in a bowl. Add black beans and cottage cheese. Add soy sauce.

Mix all the ingredients together thoroughly. Mold the mixture into bone shapes and place on a cookie sheet.

Bake for 45 minutes in a 375-degree oven. Let cool.

Boo's Biscuits

- ❖ 3 1/2 cup whole wheat flour
- ❖ 2 cup Quaker oats
- ❖ 1 cup milk
- ❖ 1/2 cup hot water
- ❖ 2 beef or chicken bouillon cubes
- ❖ 1/2 cup meat drippings

Dissolve bouillon cubes in hot water. Add milk and drippings and beat. In a separate bowl, mix flour and oatmeal. Pour liquid ingredients into dry ingredients and mix well.

Press to cookie sheets that do not feel and cut into the desired form. Bake 300 degrees for 1 hour. Turn off the heat and let the oven harden. Cool after baking.

Bow Wow Biscuits

- 2 1/2 cups whole wheat flour
- 1/2 cup wheat germ
- 1/2 cup powdered milk
- 1/2 teaspoon salt
- 1/2 teaspoon garlic powder
- 8 tablespoons bacon grease -- or margarine
- 1 egg -- beaten
- 1 teaspoon brown sugar
- 2 tablespoons beef broth -- or chicken
- 1/2 cup ice water
- 6 slices Bacon -- crumbled, optional
- 1/2 cup cheddar cheese, shredded -- optional

In a big mixing bowl, mix all ingredients thoroughly to form a dough. Roll the dough out with a rolling pin and use a cookie cutter to make shapes for cookies.

Bake cookies at 350 degrees for 20 - 25 min.

Bow Wow Burritos

- 1 tablespoon oil
- 12 ounces cooked beef -- *see Note
- 1 clove garlic -- minced
- 3 tablespoons chunky peanut butter
- 1 can sweet potatoes -- (23-oz.) drained
- 1 can black beans -- (15-oz.) rinsed
- 1 teaspoon chili powder
- 1 teaspoon cumin
- 1/2 teaspoon cinnamon
- 2 teaspoons beef bouillon -- powder
- 6 flour tortillas -- (10-inch)
- 2 tablespoons cilantro -- chopped
- 6 tablespoons cheese -- shredded
- 6 tablespoons vegetables -- *see Note

Heat the oil in a large skillet over medium heat until it is hot. Add garlic; Cook and stir 2 to 3 minutes or until the tender. Stir peanut butter, sweet potatoes and beans; Mash a little.

Add cumin, cinnamon powder and chili, bouillon beef; Mix well. Reduce heat to low; Add beef, close it, simmer 2 to 3 minutes or until it is heated, stirred occasionally.

Meanwhile, heat tortillas according to package directions. To serve, spoon, spread scant 1/2 cup mixture across center third of each tortilla with one piece of meat in center.

Top each with 1 tablespoon sour cream, 1 teaspoon cilantro, l tablespoon Cheese spread to cover mixture.

Fold sides of each tortilla 1 inch over filling. Fold bottom 1/3 of tortilla over filling; roll again to enclose filling.

*Note: Beef or chicken cut into 1/2-inch strips, or "meatless" meat for the vegetarian doggies.

*Note: Optional... Shredded veggies for added nutrition, carrots, green beans, broccoli etc.

Serving Ideas: Add one Teaspoon Dog Oil Supplement and one teaspoon Dog Powder Mix Supplement for added nutrition before folding burritos.

Bread Machine Dog Biscuits

- 3/4 cup Beef stock -- *see Note
- 1 egg
- 3 tablespoons oil
- 1 cup all-purpose flour
- 1 cup whole wheat flour
- 1/3 cup Bulgur -- *see Note
- 1/3 cup Bran
- 1/4 cup nonfat dry milk
- 1/4 teaspoon Garlic powder
- 1 1/2 teaspoons yeast

Place ingredients in bread pan according to the manufacturer's directions and press "Dough" cycle. When it sounds a beep, get rid of mixture to swallow a light countertop and with a rolling pin, roll the mixture to 1/4 "thickness with corn flour.

Re-roll memo and repeat until all the mixture is used. Place it in a warm location and let it up 30 minutes.

Bake at 325 for 30 minutes until brown and no longer soft. Place on a rack to cool. Store in an airtight container.

* Chicken, Vegetable Or use hot water and 2 or 3 -bouillon cubes.

**If you do not have bulgur try substituting something like a 7-grain cereal.

Breath Busters Biscuits

- ❖ 1 1/2 cups whole wheat flour
- ❖ 1 1/2 cups Bisquick ® baking mix
- ❖ 1/2 cup mint leaves -- loosely packed
- ❖ 1/4 cup milk
- ❖ 4 tablespoons margarine
- ❖ 1 egg
- ❖ 1 1/2 tablespoons maple syrup -- or corn syrup

Combine all the ingredients in a food processor, process to mix well, mint cut, and large ball shape. Press or roll the non-stick surface (flourboard or ceramic) to a thickness of 1/2 / 2 ".

Cut to 1x2" strip or with a bone-shaped cake cutter and place it on a non-stick cookie pan. Bake at 375 ° for 20 minutes or until browned is mild. Cool and store in air-tight container.

Makes about 30 medium biscuits.

Buddy Boys Dog Biscuits

- ❖ 1 cup whole wheat flour
- ❖ 1/2 cup all-purpose flour
- ❖ 3/4 cup nonfat dry milk powder
- ❖ 1/2 cup oats, rolled (raw) -- quick cooking
- ❖ 1/2 cup yellow cornmeal
- ❖ 1 teaspoon sugar

Cut in 1/3 short winding until mixture is rough crumbs. Stir 1 egg. Dissolve one tablespoon of instant chicken granules or the bouillon beef in 1/2 cup of water.

Stir the liquid into a flour mixture with a fork. The form of the mixture into the ball and knead the flour board for 5 minutes.

Divide ball into two and roll each part to 1/2 inch. Use Cookie Cutter or Biscuit Shape. Place 6 on the plate and microwave at 5 to 10 minutes or until firm and dry for the touch.

Turn the biscuits for 1/2 cooking time.

Bulldog Banana Bites

- 2 1/4 cups whole wheat flour
- 1/2 cup powdered milk -- nonfat
- 1 egg
- 1/3 cup banana -- ripe, mashed
- 1/4 cup vegetable oil
- 1 beef bouillon cube
- 1/2 cup water -- hot
- 1 tablespoon brown sugar

Mix all ingredients until well blended. Knead for 2 minutes on a floured surface.

Roll to 1/4 " thickness. Use a 2 ½ bone shaped cookie cutter (or any one you prefer). Bake for 30 minutes in a 300 degrees oven on ungreased cookie pans.

Bulldog Brownies

- 1/2 cup shortening
- 3 tablespoons honey
- 4 eggs
- 1 teaspoon vanilla
- 1 cup whole wheat flour
- 1/4 cup carob flour
- 1/2 teaspoon baking powder

Frosting:

- 12 ounces nonfat cream cheese
- 2 teaspoons honey

Cream shortening and honey together thoroughly.

Add remaining ingredients. Beat well. Bake in a greased cookie sheet (10x15") for 25 minutes at 350 degrees.

Cool completely.

FROSTING: Blend together the ingredients. Spread frosting over the cool brownies. Cut into 3 inch or 1 1/2-inch squares.

Canine Carrot Cookies

- 2 cups carrots -- boiled and pureed
- 2 eggs
- 2 tablespoons garlic -- minced
- 2 cups unbleached flour -- *see Note
- 1 cup rolled oats
- 1/4 cup wheat germ

*or rice flour or rye flour.

Combine carrots, eggs and garlic. Mix until smooth. Add the dry ingredients. Roll out on heavily floured surface and cut into bars or desired shapes.

Bake at 300 degrees for 45 minutes or to desired crunchiness.

The centers will continue to harden as they cool. Brush cookies with egg white before baking for a glossy finish.

Canine Cookies #1

- 1 1/2 cups whole wheat flour
- 1 cup all-purpose flour
- 1 cup powdered milk -- non-fat
- 1/3 cup bacon grease -- *see Note
- 1 egg -- lightly beaten
- 1 cup cold water

In a bowl, combine flour and milk powder. Drizzle with melted fat. Add egg and water; mix well. Gather dough into a ball. On the floured surface, pat out dough.

Roll out to 1/2-inch thickness. Cut into desired shapes. Gather up scraps of dough and repeat rolling and cutting.

Bake on ungreased baking sheets in 350-degree oven for 50 - 60 minutes or until crispy.

Note: Beef fat or Chicken fat can be used

Makes about 36 - 2 1/2-inch biscuits. Store in the fridge.

Canine Cookies #2

- 1/2 cup nonfat dry milk
- 1 egg -- well beaten
- 1 1/4 cups all-purpose flour
- 1 1/4 cups wheat flour
- 1/2 teaspoon garlic powder
- 1/2 teaspoon onion salt
- 1 1/2 teaspoons brown sugar
- 1/2 cup water
- 6 tablespoons gravy
- 2 jars baby food, meat, beef, strained

Combine ingredients and shape into ball. Roll out on floured board, use extra flour if needed. Cut with knife or cookie cutter.

Bake at 350 degrees for 25 to 30 min. Cool.

Should be quite hard.

Canine Cookies #3

- ❖ 1/2 cup dry milk
- ❖ 1 1/2 teaspoons brown sugar
- ❖ 1 egg -- well beaten
- ❖ 1/2 cup water
- ❖ 2 1/2 cups flour
- ❖ 6 tablespoons gravy
- ❖ 1/2 teaspoon garlic salt
- ❖ 1 jar baby food, meat, beef, strained -- or more if needed

Combine and shape into ball and roll-on floured board.

Use the extra flour if needed. Cut to desired shape, Bake at 350-degrees F for 25 - 30 min. Cool. Should be hard.

Canine Meat and Grain Menu

- ❖ 2 cups cooked brown rice
- ❖ 2/3 cup Lean beef
- ❖ 2 teaspoons lard -- or veggie oil
- ❖ 1/4 cup vegetables -- no onion
- ❖ Supplements*

Mix the above. You can cook the meat if you want to, use your judgment. Serve slightly warm.

*For supplements, add 2 tsp. powder and 1 tsp. oil to feed daily- now this is for a 5-15 lb. dog, and book instructs to use double supplements for a puppy.

Carob Cornered Crunchies

- 2 1/4 cups whole wheat flour
- 1 egg
- 1/4 cup applesauce
- 1/4 cup vegetable oil
- 1 beef bouillon -- or chicken
- 1/2 cup hot water
- 1 tablespoon honey
- 1 tablespoon molasses
- 1 cup carob bar -- about

Mix all ingredients together until well blended. Knead dough two minutes on a lightly floured surface. Roll to 1/4" thickness. Bake on ungreased cookie sheet for 30 minutes in a 300-degree oven. Cool.

Melt carob chips in microwave or saucepan. Dip cool biscuits in carob or lay on a flat surface and brush carob over biscuits with a pastry brush. Let cool.

Champion Cheese & Veggies Chews

- ❖ 1/2 cup grated cheese -- room temp.
- ❖ 3 tablespoons vegetable oil
- ❖ 3 teaspoons applesauce
- ❖ 1/2 cup vegetables -- what ever you like
- ❖ 1 cup whole wheat flour
- ❖ nonfat milk

Mix cheese, the oil and applesauce together. Add veggies, flour. Combine thoroughly.

Add just enough milk to help form a ball. Cover and chill for 1 hour. Roll onto a floured surface and cut into shapes. Bake in a preheated 375-degree oven 15 minutes or until golden brown.

Let cool.

Cheese and Bacon Dog Biscuits

- ❖ 3/4 cup Flour
- ❖ 1/2 teaspoon Baking Soda
- ❖ 1/2 teaspoon Salt
- ❖ 2/3 cup Butter
- ❖ 2/3 cup Brown Sugar
- ❖ 1 Egg
- ❖ 1 teaspoon Vanilla extract
- ❖ 1 1/2 cups oatmeal
- ❖ 1 cup Cheddar Cheese -- shredded
- ❖ 1/2 cup Wheat Germ
- ❖ 1/2-pound Bacon -- or bacon bits

Combine flour, soda, salt; mix well and set aside. Cream butter and sugar beat in egg and vanilla. Add flour, mix well.

Stir in oats, cheese, wheat germ and bacon. Drop by rounded tablespoon onto ungreased baking sheets. Bake at 350 for 16 minutes. Cool and let the critters enjoy!

Cheese and Garlic Dog Cookies

- 1 1/2 cups whole wheat flour
- 1 1/4 cups cheddar cheese -- grated
- 1/4-pound margarine -- corn oil
- 1 clove garlic -- crushed
- 1 Pinch salt

Cream the cheese with the softened margarine, garlic, salt, and flour. Add enough milk to form into a ball. Chill for 1/2 hour. Roll onto floured board. Cut into shapes and bake at 375 for 15 minutes or until slightly brown, and firm.

MAKES 2 to 3 dozen, depending on size.

Cheese N Garlic Bites

- 1 cup wheat flour
- 1 cup cheddar cheese -- grated
- 1 tablespoon garlic powder
- 1 tablespoon butter -- softened
- 1/2 cup milk

Mix flour and cheese together. Add garlic powder and softened butter. Slowly add milk till you form a stiff dough.

You may not need all the milk. Knead on floured board for a few minutes. Roll out to 1/4-inch thickness. Cut into shapes, place on ungreased cookie sheet.

Bake 350 degrees oven for 15 minutes. Let cool in oven with the door slightly open until cold and firm. Refrigerate to keep fresh.

Cheesey Dog Cookies

- 2 cups All-Purpose flour -- un-sifted
- 1 1/4 cups cheddar cheese -- shredded
- 2 cloves Garlic -- finely chopped
- 1/2 cup Vegetable oil
- 4 tablespoons Water -- (4 to 5)

Combine everything except water. Whisk in the food processor until consistency of cornmeal. Add water until mixture forms a ball.

Roll it into 1/2" thickness, cut into shapes. Bake on ungreased cookie sheets about 10 min. (depending on size of shapes) at 400. Cool and store in refrigerator.

Cheesy Carrot Muffins

- 1 cup all-purpose flour
- 1 cup whole wheat flour
- 1 tablespoon baking powder
- 1 cup cheddar cheese -- Shredded
- 1 cup carrot -- grated
- 2 large eggs
- 1 cup milk

Preheat oven to 350 degrees. Grease a muffin tin or line it with paper baking cups. Combine flours and baking powder and mix well. Add cheese and carrots and use your fingers to mix them into the flour until they are well-distributed. In another bowl, beat eggs. Then whisk in the milk and vegetable oil. Pour this over the flour mixture and stir gently until just combined.

Fill ¾ muffins full of mixture. Bake for 20-25 minutes or until the muffin feels chewy. Be sure to let muffin cool before leaving your dog to do a taste! One muffin for middle to large dogs, half muffins for toys or small dogs.

Chewy Cheesy Chihuahua Pizza

Crust:
- 2 cups cake flour
- 1 1/4 cups whole wheat flour
- 1/4 cup olive oil
- 1 egg
- 1 cup water
- 1 teaspoon baking soda

Sauce & Toppings:
- 1 tomato
- 1 cup tomato puree
- 1 clove garlic
- 1/4 cup parmesan cheese -- grated
- 1/2 teaspoon oregano
- 1/2 teaspoon basil
- 2/3 cup cooked rice

CRUST:

Mix all ingredients together. Knead on a lightly floured surface. Spray a regular sized, 12" pizza pan with nonstick spray.

Next, spread the dough to edges of the pan, forming a lip around the ends. Set aside.

Sauce & Toppings:
In a food processor, blend tomato, tomato puree, garlic. Spoon the mixture over the pizza crust. Sprinkle the cheese and spices evenly over sauce. Cut pizza into slices with a pizza cutter or sharp knife.

Bake in a 325-degree F oven for 25 minutes. Take out, sprinkle rice evenly over the pizza. Return to oven and bake 25 minutes more.

Yield: one 12-inch pizza.

Chicken Flavored Dog Biscuits

- 2 1/2 teaspoons dry yeast
- 1/4 cup warm water
- 1 teaspoon salt -- optional
- 1 egg
- 1 cup chicken broth -- slightly warmed
- 1 cup whole wheat flour
- 1/2 cup rye flour -- optional
- 1/2 cup cornmeal
- 1 cup cracked wheat
- 1 1/2 cups all-purpose flour

In a large bowl, dissolve yeast with warm water. Add the salt, one beaten egg, and warm chicken broth.

Add all flour except versatile flour, and then mix well. Slowly add multipurpose flour until the dough is rigid formed and can be identified by hand. Knead is only a few minutes, enough to get the mixture to unite.

Roll out dough about 1/4" thick and cut with cookie cutters, Place biscuits on a large cookie tray and place directly in a 300-degree oven, they do not need to rise. Bake for 45 min. and then turn off the oven.

You can let them sit in the oven overnight and in the morning, they will be hard and good for your dog's teeth.

You could also vary this recipe by adding milk for a milk-bone type biscuit or shortening for a little extra fat. Try different liquids and even honey or molasses.

Check with your veterinarian for other nutritional suggestions.

Chicken Garlic Birthday Cake

- ❖ 1 chicken bouillon cube
- ❖ 1 cup Whole-wheat flour
- ❖ 2 cups Wheat germ
- ❖ 1/2 cup Cornmeal
- ❖ 2 Eggs
- ❖ 1/2 cup Vegetable oil
- ❖ 1 tablespoon Minced garlic
- ❖ 2 cups water
- ❖ vegetable oil spray -- Garlic Flavor

Preheat oven to 375 degrees. Dissolve bouillon cube in warm water. Combine flour, wheat germ, cornmeal, eggs, oil, garlic, and water.

Spray two cake pans with garlic-flavored oil and sprinkle with flour. Bake for 50 minutes. After removing cake from oven, turn upside down and let cool.

MAKES two small cakes.

Chow Chow Chicken

- 2 chicken thighs -- or white meat
- 1 stalk celery -- sliced thick
- 3 carrot -- peeled and halved
- 2 small potato -- peeled and cubed
- 2 cups rice -- uncooked

Place chicken pieces in large pot. Cover with cold water (5 -6 cups). Add carrots, celery, and potatoes to water.

Add salt. Cover and simmer on low heat about 2 hours until the chicken becomes tender. Add the rice, cover, and cook over low heat for about 30 minutes until rice is tender and most of the liquid is absorbed.

Remove soup from heat. Pull the chicken meat off the bone (if will practically fall off), discard bones. Return shredded pieces to pot. Stir well.

Let cool. Store in the refrigerator or freeze.

Chow Chow Stew

- 1 tablespoon olive oil
- 2 pounds beef -- *see Note
- 2 cups cabbage -- chopped
- 3 cloves garlic -- minced, up to 4
- 18 ounces canned sweet potatoes -- drained and chopped
- 14 1/2 ounces canned tomato wedges -- undrained
- 1 1/2 cups tomato juice
- 3/4 cup apple juice
- 1 teaspoon ginger root -- up to 2, grated
- 2 cups green beans, frozen -- cut crosswise
- 1/3 cup peanut butter
- 6 cups cooked brown rice

Heat the oil in a large skillet over medium-high heat. Cook Beef, Add the cabbage and garlic; cook, stirring, until the cabbage is tender-crisp, about 5 minutes. Stir in sweet potatoes, tomatoes, tomato juice, apple juice, ginger.

Reduce heat to medium-low and then cover. Simmer until hot and bubbling, about 6 minutes.

Stir in the green beans and simmer, uncovered, for 5 minutes. Stir in the peanut butter until well-blended and hot, about one minute. Spoon over rice.

*Note: Low Fat, or use chicken, lamb, fish. Liver can be used as well.

Classic Canine Cookies

- 4 cups whole wheat flour
- 1/4 cup cornmeal
- 1/4 cup cooked rice
- 1 egg
- 2 tablespoons vegetable oil
- Juice from a small orange
- 1 2/3 cups water

Mix all ingredients together. Turn out onto the lightly floured surface and knead. Roll out dough to about 1/8-inch thickness and cut out desired shapes... doggy bones, paws, balls, etc... have fun!

Dipping Sauce:
#1

- 3 cups vanilla chips
- 1 Tbsp. spinach powder
- 1 tsp. garlic powder
- 1 tsp. vegetable oil

#2

- ❖ 3 cups carob chips
- ❖ 1 tsp. vegetable oil
- ❖ 1 tsp. turmeric powder

Melt chips in a double boiler or microwave.

Add oils and seasonings. Dip tips of cookies, when cooled, into desired sauce and place on a pan lined with wax paper until set.

Corgi Crumpets

- 2 1/2 cups cornmeal
- 1 1/2 cups cake flour
- 2 tablespoons vegetable oil
- 1 egg
- 2/3 cup honey
- 1/2 teaspoon baking powder
- 1/2 teaspoon cinnamon
- 1/2 teaspoon nutmeg
- 1 small apple
- 1 1/3 cups water
- 1/2 cup rolled oats

Preheat oven to 350. In a bowl, mix all ingredients except the apple and rolled oats. Grate apple into mixture.

With an ice cream scoop fill into muffin pans lined with paper baking cups and sprinkle with oats. Bake for 40 minutes.

Darlene's Favorite Dog Cookie

- ❖ 2 cups rye flour
- ❖ 1/2 cup vegetable oil
- ❖ 2/3 cup warm water
- ❖ 1/2 cup white flour
- ❖ 1/4 cup cornmeal

Mix well. I usually add about 1/4 tsp. either vanilla or mint flavor.

Roll out to 1/4" thick. Cut into shapes (I usually use about a 3-4" bone-shape cutter).

Bake on lightly greased cookie sheet for 30 minutes at 350 degrees.

Note

CPSIA information can be obtained
at www.ICGtesting.com
Printed in the USA
LVHW081509131221
706069LV00011B/400